TURN YOUR GAMING INTO a CAREER THROUGH TWITCH AND OTHER STREAMING SITES

HOW TO START, DEVELOP AND SUSTAIN AN ONLINE STREAMING BUSINESS THAT MAKES MONEY

Copyright © 2018

N00btoProGames.com

INTRODUCTION

Let's face it – every gamer in 2018 wants to be the next Twitch superstar. Who in their right mind wouldn't want it? The job description reads: "You will broadcast and play video games every day for hours on end and get paid to read weird messages from anonymous strangers on-screen." Isn't that awesome?

This short, but jam-packed book will unravel the mysteries and misconceptions associated with this lucrative career path. Once you finish reading it, you will be equipped with all the knowledge required to make the right choices at the right time, and avoid the common pitfalls and traps along the road.

TABLE OF CONTENTS

LEGAL NOTES

Add any legal disclaimers here.

WHAT YOU NEED TO GET STARTED

If you are serious about embarking on a Twitch streaming career path, setting up a proper, dedicated space for streaming in your house or apartment is necessary before anything else.

THE PC

First, let us talk briefly about your PC, the "engine" below the hood. Obviously, if you are a gamer, you already have the machine ready to fire.

As with any machine, your PC requires minimum maintenance and care in order to run well. If you do not use liquid cooling, make sure you do not cram it somewhere in the corner with no airflow. Install MSI Afterburner to monitor your CPU and GPU temperature. You do not want to fry your circuitry on a hot summer day. If you live in a particularly humid area, you might want to consider investing in a dehumidifier.

Know the limits of your setup and do not abuse it. After all, your career will overwhelmingly depend on the state of your equipment.

MICROPHONES, HEADSETS, KEYBOARDS, MICE

While we are on the topic of equipment, let us cover the crucial accessories. First, the microphone. If you are really, really, short on cash flow, sure, you can temporarily get by using the microphone from your headset, or that cheap one you got from the grandma for your 12th birthday. However, you should really consider investing in a proper microphone that will not sound like you are making sounds out of a meat grinder.

As with most anything these days, there are countless options out there. However, select few rise above the rest. Here are a few recommendations:

1. The budget option: Zalman ZM-Mic1

For about $10, this compact little microphone will clip onto your headset cord and provide a substantial upgrade in sound fidelity. It is not super awesome, but considering how cheap it is, it is a perfect Band-Aid fix for horrible static noise and other issues commonly found in headset mics. It does pick up quite a bit of background noise, but if you are in a quiet room, it is hardly even noticeable.

2. Anywhere you go: Samson Portable Go Mic

This nifty little device is seriously underrated. The overwhelmingly positive customer feedback speaks for itself. Price, quality, versatility and most of all fidelity are all up to par with even the more expensive options out there. If you want a multi-purpose solution that will serve you well in all kinds of situations, this is it.

3. Bang for a buck: Blue Yeti

The Holy Grail, the crème de la crop of sound fidelity and adaptability for often times half the price of alternative options. You can place it just about anywhere it will still pick up your voice just fine. Yes, it will still pick up keyboard and mouse clicks when placed directly on the table. If you are really annoyed by it, you can put some kind of a cushion or foam beneath it to dampen the vibrations. Overall, this is by far the best pick for any up-and-coming streamer who doesn't want to break the bank.

Furthermore, owning a proper combination of a headset, keyboard and mouse is vital primarily for the longevity of your Twitch career. Think about it - you will be spending hours, days, WEEKS wearing those bulky headsets, mashing WASD on the keyboard and left-clicking your mouse into oblivion.

That's why these accessories have to be both sturdy and comfortable to use. Due to the vast size and shape differences, no headset will fit every head comfortably and no mouse or keyboard is going to suit every pair of hands out there.

Still, here are a couple recommendations for you to check out:

HEADSETS

1. The futuristic hobo: BENGOO G9000
2. The intermediate: HyperX Cloud II
3. Up there with the best: Sennheiser GAME ZERO/GAME ONE

KEYBOARDS

1. Too good to be true? Turtle Beach Impact 100
2. The mechanical marvel: Razer BlackWidow Chroma
3. Wireless wizardry: Logitech G613 LIGHTSPEED

MICE

1. Cheapskate solution: Logitech G300s
2. Hefty lefty: SteelSeries Sensei 310 (I personally use this one)
3. Perfect for just about anything: Logitech G502 Proteus Spectrum

INTERNET CONNECTION

Internet connection is the lifeblood of your Twitch stream. Without a proper online access in place, none of your fancy equipment will matter. At the very minimum, you want your upload speed to be at least 5 mbit/s (megabits per second). However, if you want to broadcast a high-quality stream while simultaneously enjoying a lag-less gaming experience yourself, don't go below 10 mbit/s.

Depending on the game and the broadcasting resolution, each game will behave differently. Dynamic games can look like crap at 720p and a bitrate of 3.5 mbit/s, while slower and more stationary ones will look just fine sitting at 2 mbit/s 1080p. You will have to test each game individually to figure out the best settings, which is why having a decent upload speed will help you dial the bitrates up or down, depending on the circumstances.

STREAMING SOFTWARE

There are really only two choices here – **Open Broadcast Software(OBS)** & **XSplit**. 9 out of 10 times you will want to use OBS. It's very easy to use, stable, performs very well and it costs nothing. Best of all, it's very well documented online, with dozens of videos, tutorials and troubleshooting solutions to get you on your way.

Meanwhile, XSplit is only worthwhile if you'll use the premium version with all of its extra features, as the free version has very limited functionality. Even then, it only comes into play with a bit more complicated setups (multiple channels, Skype video feeds, tournaments, casters etc.)

In most cases, it's best to save the money and go OBS all the way.

SCHEDULING

As a new streamer on the scene, you will really want to schedule your future streams in advance. We humans are creatures of habit, and what better way to serve your human viewers than to establish a reliable timetable of live broadcasts.

Think of it this way. Your viewers are the consumers of your product. You are in the business of serving them their daily dose of entertainment. At the very least, you can serve them by establishing a routine delivery of said entertainment. The success is built on countless small steps. Having a streaming schedule you adhere to rigorously and religiously is the first step in that direction.

How to Establish a Unique Identity and Brand

Now that you've got all the basics covered, let's talk about your style, your personality, your identity, your brand!

You may wonder, what is a brand anyway? Put simply, a brand is associated with a distinct name, identity, design, symbolism and characteristics of a specific product or service.

When you see an iPhone, you instantly associate it with Apple and Steve Jobs. When you see a DualShock controller, you instantly associate it with PlayStation and Sony. When you see a familiar purple Glitch icon, you instantly associate it with Twitch.

Every single successful Twitch streamer has a brand. Things they do, phrases and punch-lines they're known for, games they play, the style and color scheme of their overlay, custom emoticons, memes... These are all elements of a brand.

This is why it is of utmost importance for you to start developing and establishing your brand from day 1. Let's explore some options for building a brand.

ALTER-EGO

Dr Disrespect. The man, the myth, the legend. Anybody who's hopped around Twitch has at least heard about the Doc. Everything about this wildly successful streamer is over-the-top, yet that's exactly the formula he used to become a Twitch phenomenon.

Now, you obviously won't have to or even be able to go to such a length in order to have a successful Twitch career. However, it's important to understand just how powerful adopting a specific persona and playing a role can be.

Basically, you have to find a way to stand out from the rest of the new streamers out there. Obviously, if you are exceptionally skilled at a popular game, people will naturally gravitate towards your stream. There are scores of ex-pros who have found their way to Twitch success based solely on their ability to pull off insane plays over and over again. Even their fans will often admit their streams are just boring and they are being watched only because they're good at the game.

But, if you're not particularly good at any game out there, you'll have to start pulling out rabbits out of the hat. Well, sort of. The facial expressions, the jokes, the phrases, the toys in the background, the pet cat that jumps on the keyboard and results in hilarious fails - everything about you and around you can become a part of your online persona. You don't have to force these things, but be mindful of their influence and importance.

DESIGN

There's no need to spend a lot of time poring over your overlay design, but it still matters, so it should be dealt with accordingly.

The easiest and best route is to simply outsource it. There are professional services out there which can help you get set up very quickly, and paying for such services will hardly break the bank. However, if you are still constrained by the budget limitations and are willing to spend a few hours, you can certainly do it yourself.

If you've never dabbled with image manipulating and digital design software, there's a great online tool called Canva with tons of templates you can use to jump-start the process. You can use these however you like, but it is best if you create something simple and minimalistic. The last thing you want is a cluttered abomination that takes up more than half of your screen. For colors, it doesn't take much googling around to figure out the best combinations. Bonus points if you can make it look slick and fancy though.

Make sure you check out the logo templates specifically. Make a shortlist of the ones you like the best. Don't be afraid to ask a friend or a cousin for a second opinion. Once you've settled on the template, edit it to match your brand name and identity. It's best if you keep it same or at least similar to your overlay design. You will use this logo on your Twitter profile, Facebook page, Twitch, YouTube channel etc. The logo is now part of your brand. This is super important. The worst thing you can do is have different avatars and profile images on your social media channels. Once you adopt a certain style, be consistent with your brand design and overall image across the board.

GAME SELECTION

As a rule of thumb, new streamers find it easier to break through that first barrier of growth if they brand their stream around 1 specific game (usually the newly released title) or several similar games within the same genre (battle royale games like H1Z1, PUBG and Fortnite, for instance). Therefore, if you want to optimize your branding efforts and grow your Twitch channel at a faster rate, pick 1 game or 1 genre and stick with it. There's no shortage of new games coming out these days. Choose one and start streaming it from day 1.

However, if you enjoy a wide range of games and don't want fancy changing your gaming habits, then you will have to brand yourself as a variety streamer. Your brand will revolve primarily around your persona and your showmanship skills. It's a perfectly valid path to success. It just might take a bit more time, effort and creativity on your part to pull it off.

TWITCH PROFILE INFORMATION

By now, you've surely noticed that all Twitch streamers worth their weight have a neat and well laid-out profile information section. It usually contains some personal info mixed with information on sponsors, equipment, games they play, links to social media channels, and the schedule.

This section is the perfect spot to tell a little bit about yourself, your life and the kind of streamer you are. You can list your favourite games, movies, your wish-list, life goals etc. Above all, it's the perfect spot to provide scheduling info for your viewers.

We've already touched on the importance of having a schedule. Putting your schedule on display is actually really crucial, especially early on. Don't be afraid to include it in your stream overlay and social media banners. Ask your viewers to follow you on Twitter as well and announce your streams an hour before you start broadcasting.

Surely, you get the gist of it by now. Whenever and wherever you are, if the opportunity presents itself, emphasize your streaming schedule. Pick your time slot and stick with it. Become THAT guy that streams every day from 5-11 PM!

SETTINGS THINGS IN MOTION – BUILD A STREAM

PREPARATIONS AND PLANNING

After you've purchased all the equipment and figured out what kind of entertainment you're going to be providing, it's time to actually start doing it. However, you can't just go into it willy-nilly, improvise and "wing it". Minimum planning and preparations are necessary beforehand to have an entertaining stream. It may sound weird, but you'll have to aim for a certain level of order and professionalism right from the get go.

What is the overall idea and the goal of the stream? How to present yourself? Are you confident showing your face to everyone? What are the rules? What kinds of behaviours are not welcome? How to keep things in-check once you grow to a certain level?

You will need to come up with the answers to all these questions. Prepare accordingly and plan ahead.

Webcam and Workspace

Webcam

First of all, let's talk about the webcam. The majority of successful streamers out there use one. Twitch is a live, interactive audio-visual experience. Most viewers are NOT there to watch the gameplay itself – there is YouTube for that. They want to watch a show, they want to be entertained.

That's why showing your face to the world is the better option in most cases. Even if your facial features are oddly unattractive, it's still better to present a talking head to your viewers, instead of a voice belonging to an unknown person. It humanizes your Twitch channel. Your stream and your brand identity are not just a carefully crafted collection of graphics and sounds. They belong to a real, live human being. This instantly boosts your appeal and lowers the barriers of online interaction.

On the other hand, having a webcam on and exposing a small part of your every-day life and reality to everybody willing to watch it presents its own challenges.

Workspace

There are certainly a few messy streamers out there. You probably know the type. They usually have untidy rooms, beds, empty cans and bottles laying around, bunch of stuff on the table, sometimes even to the level of actually blocking the web-camera. Even if these bad habits stunted their growth, they did not stop the growth of their channels completely.

However, rest assured that these practices will drive some of your viewers away from your stream. Chances are, nobody or very few people will care about your squeaky clean floor and all your stuff being in perfect order. But, everybody will notice the stains on your shirt, the unkempt bed and junk lying around on the floor.

So, just to be on the safe side, it won't hurt to clean up a bit before each streaming session. You want everybody who comes by your stream to focus on the show, not on the disorder and messy appearance of your room. That said, the background can also be an important part of your stream too.

For example, having a guitar positioned visibly on the stand behind your bed or sofa will pique the curiosity of your viewers, especially those that play a guitar or some other music interest. They may wonder "How good is she/he at that thing?" They may even ask you to play a few songs on it.

Obviously, everybody on Twitch is a gamer, so putting up your impressive collection of video games on display is almost a no-brainer. If you own a collection of toys, action figures, board-games and other geeky/nerdy things, make it clearly visible in the background. This is a common tactic used by many

Twitch streamers and YouTubers, and it's a one that works like a charm every time.

It's also important that you prepare enough water and snacks beforehand, especially if you live alone. You will be talking a lot and it will dry your mouth and throat very often. Snacks are always good to have around as well. You will need every ounce of energy you can get, because being an active, engaged streamer for hours on end actually requires a surprising amount of energy.

THE CHAT ENVIRONMENT

THE RULES

You probably won't have to police your Twitch chat early on, but it is still recommended to devise crystal clear rules of conduct as soon as possible.

This is the step where it's really prudent checking out bigger, more established streamers out there. They've already had to deal with all the chat problems you are dealing with currently, or will have to in the future. Check out their info section and look for chat/behaviour rules.

Obviously, some things are auto-include, but there are always nuances, of course. Racism, bullying and sexism belong in this category. Will you adopt a zero-tolerance policy, or will you be just a bit more lenient towards an occasional joke with racial and sexual undertones? This is important when it comes to underage viewers. You will simply have to be careful not exposing this demographic to anything that can get you in trouble with their parents, so be extra careful with any external links in chat or in your notifications.

Cursing, rude behaviour and ALL CAPS can be a problem too. If you tend to drop F-bombs yourself, your viewers will naturally feel more inclined to do the same in chat. How far are you willing to let it go then? Things can escalate quickly under the guise of online anonymity. It is best to keep it at minimum, or if you don't want to find yourself on a slippery slope, just refrain from foul language yourself and don't allow it in chat too.

Trolls are inevitable, even your "good citizens" might turn up rowdy sometimes. Where do you draw the line? How much is too much? This is, again, why it's best to just blanket-ban any links in chat, except for chat moderators and yourself of course. You don't want to be overly restrictive, because nobody will engage in chat then, but draw a strict line and don't let anybody step over it. No exceptions.

TWITCH CHATBOTS

The bots are your first line of defence against rules breakers. At first, you probably won't even need one. You will be able to do things manually for a while, and it will help you establish direct relationship with your first few viewers. Still, it is best to take care of this part sooner rather than later. You want to be ready to put out flames before they turn into wildfires.

So, in case you don't know, let's see what exactly these bots are good for. Among others, here is the list of things these nifty little programs can help you with:

- Automatically time-out users if they use offensive words or exhibit prohibited behavior in chat

- Create custom chat commands to provide information and answer frequent questions posted in chat

- Auto-messages every once in a while (promote your merchandise; ask for follows on social media channels etc.)

- Automatically delete all messages containing links (exceptions allowed)

- Play music (song request feature)

- Organize chat mini-games/raffles

If you're not sure which one to choose, Moobot, Nightbot or Streamlabs Chatbot are perfectly suited for beginners and veterans alike. They have similar features, they are relatively simple and are used by a lot of streamers out there. Most importantly, they're under constant development, coming with improved features and increased stability with each new version.

Obviously, the bots do not possess any levels of AI to discern between an offender and someone who has a genuine interest in sharing something in chat and/or with you. Their feature lists are impressive, but they're designed to handle boatloads of menial, simple tasks. Don't go full control-freak mode and dominate your chat with the bots. Your chat moderators are there to ensure peace and order as well.

CHAT MODERATORS

Speaking of chat moderators, they're a vital part of your streaming experience. Having one or a few is not an immediate necessity. You can pretty much handle things yourself using chat-bots like Moobot or Nightbot for a while. However, as soon as you start hitting 100+ concurrent viewers, things become complicated fast.

Juggling between playing the game and engaging with the chat becomes increasingly overwhelming as your numbers grow. Your Twitch chat will become a livelier place, and a few individuals will stand out. They will be more engaged and, most importantly, some of them will turn out to be trustworthy. Cue your first chat moderator (simply known as "mods") candidates.

Trust is the first and most important prerequisite. While you're playing and focusing on the game, you need to have absolute confidence your chat mods will enforce the rules and interact with other chat participants for you. For example, there will be situations where chatbots won't be able to handle the issues or fulfil requests. This is where mods come in to save the day.

Here are a couple of guidelines to help you choose the right person for the job:

- she/he has been around in chat for a few months at least
- cool-headed, rational and mature approach to most situations
- knows and follows the rules of the chat herself/himself

- has patience for newcomers and is willing to help out when asked to
- contributes to the chat culture and quality with insightful, polite and/or funny comments
- commands a certain level of respect from other chat participants
- sees eye-to-eye with your own vision of the stream, community culture and chat environment

Most chat mods are volunteers who do the job for free. Treat them with respect they deserve for helping you out and interact in a collaborative way. Yes, it's your stream and yes, you have the last word, but if you delegate certain portion of the workload to another person, that person becomes a vital contributor to the show herself/himself. That's why it's perfectly reasonable and within your right to treat your mods with special, mod-only privileges and rewards for their continued support. Send them tangibles – T-shirts, jugs or gaming accessories, for example. If you have some extra time and can align your schedule with them, invite them for private gaming session in your favourite game. Hell, if you live close-by, you can even meet up for a LAN party. Remember their birthdays, send a custom "thank you" card. They'll love and appreciate the gesture. They're always there for you, so when you can, be there for them.

This is why it's important to be on the same page regarding everything. Discuss your views and expectations about the stream and chat with them.

Let them express their own ideas if they have any. Maybe you are a bit more open-minded or vice-versa when it comes to certain topics. Then, how do you want that person to handle the situation where the issue is somehow correlated with the difference in views?

For example, maybe you don't want to be so harsh to trolls in certain situations. Tell your mods what these situations are so they can handle them better the next time issue pops up. Spam and large blocks of text are another gray area. If somebody does it just here and there, you might want to keep that person engaged in chat regardless. However, how much is too much? You will have to discuss this and come up with a mutually agreeable decision regarding these issues.

Now, your chat mods have their lives too. They have families, jobs and other duties they need to attend to. Maybe they aren't available every time you stream. This is why it's important to always have a few "backup" mods ready to jump in when your "default" ones are not around. Obviously, it's best if you can just rely on your regular team of mods all the time, but life happens and you need to be prepared for unforeseen circumstances, just in case.

Last, but not least, don't let your mods take over the chat. Having too many active moderators can be equally problematic as well as having too few. You'll also want to keep an eye on your mods as well. Power-hungry mods who abuse their rights, privileges and think they are above the rules can quickly ruin your chat atmosphere. Listen to your regular viewers, if they complain about a certain mod, don't be afraid to demote him/her.

Ultimately, you are there to please the Average Twitch Joe, so do your best to do just that.

STREAMING ADVICE – TIPS FOR A BETTER STREAM

THE PURPOSE OF YOUR STREAM

It goes without saying that something motivated you to become a Twitch streamer. The fact that you are reading these lines means you see it as something more than a side hobby.

Ask yourself, why do you want to become a successful Twitch streamer? Do you see it as a valid career path? Are you in it to make new friendships and connections? Or maybe you just want to become Twitch famous and make money in the process?

What will your stream offer to the viewers? Will it be an entertaining daily show, or a demonstration of your ungodly skills? Will you provide certain insight into the games you play or activities you do, like 3D art or modelling? How do you actually plan on presenting yourself and your stream?

These are all questions that need to be answered if you want to maximize your chances for success and make your stream as awesome as possible. You need to know the "why" and "how".

THE PERFECT NICHE FOR YOU

Depending on the unique set of personality traits and skills you posses, your optimal pathway to Twitch success differs from everybody else. The differences might be small, but they are there. Consider them as opportunities to stand out from the rest of the up and coming Twitch streamers.

Basically, you will need to observe and detect untapped territory and conquer it before everybody else. Possibilities are literally endless. The choice of a game or a genre is only the tip of the iceberg. Pets, toys, room lightning, clothes, thematic atmosphere, cheesy tropes, unconventional play-styles, acting out an over-the-top persona, punch-lines, phrases, unique follower & subscriber callouts, dance moves, facial expressions, ridiculous ideas and encounters in-game, artistic skills... You catch the drift here, I hope.

Even if nothing original and unique pops to your mind at the moment, it's enough to borrow some practice or routine from another streamer and mould it enough to make it your own. After all, no idea is truly original. The endless versions and iterations of the core principle make it stand out each and every time. Capitalize on this.

REMAIN PATIENT AND LEVEL-HEADED

Once you start out, you will most likely find yourself in a seemingly stuck position. You can get a friend of yours to watch your stream, a few people may come by and leave, and you may even get a sudden surge of new viewers if you get "raided" by another streamer. However, things seem to fall back to a dead spot every time.

This is a challenge every streamer was faced with at the beginning. Forget about thousands, hundreds or even just a few dozen concurrent viewers. The challenge will be to get even 1 to stick at first, no matter what you do.

Of course, if you own a large following on another platform (YouTube, Facebook, even Twitter), you will get a few viewers every time, but the numbers won't grow that fast either.

Don't get discouraged. There's no such thing as overnight success on Twitch, or anywhere for that matter. Even streamers that have seemingly suddenly blown up have been working through their initial low-number stages for months, if not years. The sooner you stop worrying about it, the shorter this period will last.

There's another side to this story as well. Once you start growing and advancing your channel, it's important to stay grounded. Too many streamers have fallen victim to premature "fame" and "stardom".

All of a sudden, they become known in their own microcosm and it gets into their heads. They change their behaviour and their ego grows out of proportion.

Depending on the demographic you attract, this might not even be a bad thing in certain cases. More often than not though, this is a recipe for disaster. At best, you will plateau much earlier than you should have.

Bottom line is, whatever the state of your stream, your concurrent viewers, your audience, your chat and your following is, don't get emotionally or mentally invested in it. Don't despair if things aren't moving as fast as you'd want them to. But, once the situation improves, stay humble and grounded. After all, it's just numbers.

Cherish new arrivals like gold

There is one thing that will invariably help you pull yourself out from the back of line. You should acknowledge every new viewer and try to establish connections on an individual level early on. When you see that red 0 turn to 1, the best thing to do seize the moment and say something like: "Hello you beautiful human being on the other end of the line, what is your name and how is your day today?" If the person types a reply in chat, don't waste a moment, say: "Right. And who or what do I have to thank for being blessed by your presence today?"

Break the ice, make it light-hearted and funny, ease the tension and exude relaxed vibes. It really doesn't take much to lure people into your world and buy into the shared experience. Chances are, the viewer you are now talking to on a personal level is there because she/he is bored, tired from work, or just killing some time while waiting for a bus or a friend. By doing something of the extent described above, you are breaking your way into that person mind-space. You engage with her or him on a personal level, it feels organic and spontaneous

Even if you are a socially awkward weirdo, do it anyway. You might awkwardly stutter your way through the exchange, but it's a conversation nevertheless, no matter how cringey it may turn out in the end. And who knows, that person might find you even more interesting to watch for your obvious flaws and quirks.

Another important aspect to acknowledge and celebrate are followers. As much as your viewers and chat participants are valuable, your followers are the foundation upon which you can build and develop your stream beyond its current state. By clicking that follow button, these people basically say: "I like you, I like your stream, I'm willing to include you in my own reality from now on and come back for more the next time you start streaming." You can even consider it some kind of transaction. You've provided a service, and you've earned a small amount of digital "currency" for that service.

Make sure you have your alert system properly set up to notify you every time someone follows you while you are live. You should call out the person in question and welcome them. It doesn't hurt to come up with the name for your followers. You can never go wrong by calling your followers the YOUR_TWITCH_NAME Gang, but if you're a bit more creative, I'm sure you can come up with something much more witty and catchy.

If you decide to accept donations from your viewers and followers early on, don't be afraid to make it into a proper spectacle if such an event occurs. In the state where you are objectively struggling to simply capture the attention of a few souls that decide to come by your stream, even a $1 donation is a special occasion. Fire up all the horns, overload the memes flying all over the screen, induct that person into your stream's hall of fame. Do anything and everything to make it clear you appreciate someone not only paying you a visit, but a bit if money out of their pockets as well.

Bottom line is, you have to pave the way towards a stable and loyal fanbase. Not everybody will respond, but those who do will come back for more, because they've bought into your unique streaming experience.

BE CALM AND COLLECTED

Plain and simple, getting easily frustrated and throwing tantrums every time something annoying or negative happens is counter-productive. Unless you have specifically decided to adopt a persona of someone who is constantly angry and/or frustrated, ignore the little annoyances and irritations as best as you can. Don't get me wrong, the comedic value of such an approach can certainly be quite high if executed properly. After all, it's how boogie2988 became known. And this, of course.

However, not being in control of your own emotions and letting external influences shape your psychological state is a problem you need to fix in general. You really don't want to overreact on stream every time someone kills you in-game, or a troll comes by and start polluting your chat. This will only help induce the negative feedback loop, putting you in "tilt" mode and attracting even more trolls and spammers.

There's a secondary, less obvious benefit of exuding a cool-headed demeanour. It subconsciously communicates a level of authority and maturity to your audience. It's a mark of a person in charge, someone who keeps everything under control. Most people are followers, so your calmness will appear magnetic, almost mesmerizing to them. And having an extra tool for luring in viewers on your belt is always welcome.

EXERCISE, NUTRITION AND RELAXATION

Sitting in front of the screen every day for hours on end doesn't do your physical and mental health any good. In fact, it's quite detrimental. Therefore, it's important to balance your streaming efforts with proper amounts of physical exercise and rest.

If you have a day job and family duties, you might find yourself in a crunch though. Going to the gym takes time, the time you don't really have. In that case, your best option is to build your own home gym. You'll need some space, of course. Garage or a corner in your guest bedroom will do. Don't overspend on equipment. Used barbells and weights on a power-rack will do just fine. For cardio exercise, get a the most basic treadmill, or a bike if you have busted knees.

Then, download a 5x5 app on your Android or Apple smartphone and follow the routines. Trust me, you'll be amazed at just how much progress you can make using 5 simple compound exercises 3 times a week, combined with 15-30 minutes of cardio. Most importantly, you will feel so much better and have much more willpower and energy to work through your job and your regular streaming sessions.

Healthy food helps out too. If you are overweight, the "easiest" route is to switch to a keto diet. You will still be able to enjoy tasty meat, eggs and bacon, but your pastas, pizzas and rice will have to go out of the window. If you have never been in ketosis before, it's best to plan the switch from a carb-heavy to a keto diet over the weekend. You might feel a bit weak and groggy, but Friday afternoon, and then the whole Saturday and Sunday will be enough to get used to this metabolic switch.

Listening to relaxing music and meditating can help maintain the peace of your mind. This goes hand in hand with the previous point about having a calm and collected approach when dealing with issues, problems and challenges. Between your off-stream and on-stream duties, you will easily find yourself having 15+ hour workdays. Having your brain switched on in full capacity like that every day will quickly drain your focus and willpower reserves. So, turn on some chill tunes and spend some alone-time in the dark room. You want to preserve your mental health just as much as physical one.

Finally, you need to rest as well. Sleep is super important. If you don't get, at the barest minimum, 6 hours of sleep every day, you are slowly, but surely killing your body. To be on the safe side, 8 hours of sleep is recommended. However, life interferes very often. Your newborn wakes you up during night, maybe you have to tend to a sick parent every night, your job has you waking up every morning at 4am and so on.

There are plenty of interferences that can ruin your sleep, so if you can't get a decent amount of it overnight and you don't have too much time left for streaming, develop a power napping habit. Just laying down for 10-20 minutes in a semi-dreamy (hypnagogia) state will do wonders to you, trust me.

Watch your own streams

Everybody makes mistakes, especially when just starting out. The challenge is identifying your erroneous ways and figuring out ways to avoid them in the future. When you are playing a game and streaming it at the same time, you get caught up in the heat of the moment and you are most likely not even aware of all the little issues, flaws and kinks that come up during the stream.

If you feel like you are not objective towards yourself, ask a friend to provide her/his second opinion. Make a list of both the positive and negative things that come up. Obviously, this will take quite a lot of time, but it's going to provide you with a very valuable insight and data for future reference. You will be surprised just how much issues you can find even on your own, just by watching your past streams. It's an invaluable and eye-opening learning experience.

There's always room for improvement. You should strive to improve the quality and entertainment value of your stream all the time. So, what better way than to meticulously study and analyze your streams? Observe and note down things that work and improve upon those which don't.

Avoid viewbots at all costs

As with any system based on numbers, Twitch is no exception to cheating attempts. The most common and popular one are viewbots. This forbidden and frowned-upon practice has stirred up countless drama, with many big names caught up in the whirlpool of suspicious behaviour and questionable accusations.

When all is said and done, viewbotting will always turn out detrimental to your long term growth and success. A new channel with hundreds of views reeks of fraud and cheating, something that Twitch community itself is not really fond of.

You might be tired of your low concurrent viewcount now, but you really have to ask yourself if it's worth artificially inflating it at all. Yes, you will burst out to the top of your game category, which will in turn draw a few curious new eyeballs. However, as soon as your few real viewers notice no or very little activity in chat, they'll figure out what's really going on. You can almost count on somebody reporting your stream sooner or later. And then, after you get banned, all your hard work and efforts will be in vain.

Even if you somehow miraculously survive the Twitch "inquisition", the word will get out and your reputation will be tarnished forever. Kiss those sponsorship deals and early-beta opportunities goodbye. No serious entity will want to risk their own reputation by associating itself with a known offender.

Now, after viewbotting took Twitch by storm, the security and detection systems in place have been heavily improved to combat the issue. The issue is what to do when somebody else targets your channel, because you are pretty much GUARANTEED to get detected. If such a situation occurs, report it to Twitch immediately. Think about it - somebody decided to mess with your work. Twitch staff needs to be made aware of it. After all, it's your responsibility to protect and defend your channel as best as you can. When somebody puts it in jeopardy, you are well within your right to ring all the alarms at your disposal.

However, viewbotting is not the only way to cheat, after all. You may be tempted, but be aware of one thing. There are no shortcuts and "hacks" to success. Work your way up the legitimate way and you will be rewarded for your efforts sooner or later. Think long-term at all times, cut the noise and focus on your craft.

INTERACT AND ENGAGE

Leaving this for the end doesn't make it any less important. In fact, this is arguably the most important and crucial point. There's a really good reason why *"Always be talking"* is the mantra all the top streamers swear by. You are not just a pair of eyes glued to the screen. You are a living, breathing person willing to show a piece of her/his reality and life to the world. You need to communicate with whoever comes by and checks you out.

We've already covered the part about welcoming new viewers & followers and establishing rapport with them. It's even more important to nudge them into actively engaging with your stream on their own. You and your chat mods can't initiate responses all the time. You need to set up "lures" and turn those passive lurkers into active chatters.

The bait can be anything. A witty stream title, a riddle, a chat mini-game, a poll, a small reward etc. There's no shortage of options, tools and resources at your disposal you can use to direct your viewers into an interactive experience. Otherwise, what's the difference between watching a generic YouTube gameplay video and your stream then, right?

Now, let's talk about funny stuff a little bit. Cracking jokes and pulling off silly antics on stream or in-game is a timeless strategy to capture attention and make people laugh. If you are not sprinkling at least a bit of humour throughout your stream, you are really selling yourself short and doing a disservice to your viewers.

It's really not that hard to make people laugh. A bit of self-deprecation, sarcasm and irony at the right moment, cracking a joke here and there, playfully faking an exaggerated reaction to something in the moment, or imitating another streamer in a good spirit. If you have a knack for it, you can even do awkward and weird stuff, or adopt an over-the-top demeanour. Remember the real-life situations where you made a room full of people laugh their faces off. Tell a short story about it. There are a million and one funny things to do. Figure out what ticks your audience the most and ride along.

Work Through a Network, Expand Your Brand

Here's the real kicker. All of the things described above matter, but there's one thing which can almost guarantee growth and success. That is networking - building real, genuine connections with other streamers. It might look like a scary proposition, but it is probably the best way to get yourself exposed to more eyeballs quickly and easily. Droves of small streamers build off of each other's streams. You should seek to do the same yourself.

FIND THE RIGHT PARTNERS

Theoretically, it is possible you work your way into the inner circle of a very popular Twitch streamer and expose yourself to a vast audience of potential viewers. However, this is quite unlikely and frankly, it's ethically questionable behaviour if you are "fishing" for viewers this way. First of all, big streamers are usually more interested in playing with other big streamers. They might even find your interesting and funny, but they gain little to no benefit from collaborating with you. Exceptions exist, but they are just that, exceptions.

Instead, direct your efforts towards other streamers that have similar reach and following like you. If you have a few hundred followers, 200 for example, and just a handful of concurrent viewers on most days, then someone with 300-400 followers and a wee bit more concurrent viewers is a much better match for you than streamers with thousands of followers and hundreds of viewers. Browse through the category corresponding with your game/activity of choice and see if there are any streamers that match the criteria. Check them out and see if you fancy their first impression, and whether their stream is of an acceptable quality and value to you.

If the answer is yes, do not ask for collaboration right away. Obviously, don't just blatantly advertise your own stream in their chat either. If you wonder why, put yourself in their position. Imagine if someone you never met or talked to suddenly appears out of nowhere and tries to persuade you into doing something. You'd be naturally suspicious and unwilling to commit. That's why it's rarely a good move to start throwing collaboration requests in their faces right away.

The best and most natural way to do this is to establish a meaningful relationship and gain the streamer's trust. Spend some time in their chat, get to know the person, figure out whether that person's play-style and stream culture is even compatible with yours. Don't just blindly chase the numbers. Figure out whether the streamer brings any additional quality and entertainment value to your own viewers. Maybe she or he is a very quiet and withdrawn person. You on the other hand, are quite energetic and straightforward. Will you styles mesh well together, or will it be an awkward meeting of two vastly different souls?

Don't forget that's it's a two-way street though. In order to get something out of it, you have to bring something to the table as well. As you watch and interact with the streamer, write small notes along the way and figure out what additional quality and value you yourself can provide to their stream.

Bottom line is, the two of you need to be sufficiently compatible in order for this to work. Otherwise, you'll be doing yourself, your stream and your viewers a big disservice if you are only after the numbers and new viewers.

THE SHARED EXPERIENCE

Often times in work and in life in general, the whole is more than the sum of its parts. The same applies to collaborating with other streamers. The two of you together create something new, something that's not possible to create by either of you on your own. This, of course, can work in your favour, but it can also be detrimental. It is therefore of utmost importance to properly "scout" and "screen" the streamers you consider collaborating with in advance, as described above.

So, how can 2 or more streamers together create something more special than each one individually? The answer lies in the synergy and complementary skill-sets and abilities. For instance, you might be an outgoing person who engages with your viewers and the chat on a regular basis, but don't pay much attention to the game. In your case, somebody who is a bit quieter and tends to pay more attention to the game than the stream might actually be a perfect choice. You will fill in for his lack of direct engagement, and she or he will help you out not be terrible in the game.

Another example might be the jokester and the mad, angry streamer who is constantly salty. While the jokester is cracking jokes and laughing his face off all the time, the mad guy or gal is comically annoyed by all the randomness, chaos and/or fails in-game. Of course, this is more of an act than a real thing (remember, calm and collected, right?) but it works surprisingly well every time. Basically, aim to provide value to your partner's stream. Don't take it for granted and treat it with a "What's in it for me?" attitude.

If you play your cards right, you can reasonably expect your partner to host your stream once she/he goes offline or on days when she/he is not streaming. Seize those opportunities and say hello to her/his viewers. Let them know the rules of your own stream and briefly describe what you're doing at the moment. Remember, always keep talking, you want everybody to feel welcome, motivated to come over to your channel, participate in chat and hopefully follow you as well.

The smart people working at Twitch have realized the massive brand building potential of streamers working together. This is why there are official Twitch teams. These are basically groups of streamers that work and stream together, usually sharing compatible play-styles and similar streaming goals. Becoming a Twitch team member is one of the best ways to get the initial push. For that to happen, you need to have a network of relationships and connections with other streamers. Let's talk about how to develop one.

NETWORKING

As with anything in business and in life, the more people in the industry you know and know you, the more opportunities will present themselves to you. You can have the best gear, the most awesome graphics, sound-bites and overlays and the most amazing routine, but on your own, the growth and progress of your Twitch channel will be much slower.

Therefore, participating in the community during your offline hours is basically a must these days. You will have to put effort into getting to know the prominent community members, Twitch staff and your most active and engaged viewers. An important caveat though – don't do this for the selfish reasons. Sooner or later, people will see through your self-centred mindset. Instead, become genuinely invested and engaged in cultivating meaningful relations with the people in question. This is easier said than done when you are often preoccupied with your own stream, but try to strive towards continued improvement both on Twitch and in real life.

In return, you can expect other people to treat you the same as well. Having somebody else promote your brand, stream with you and even host you on their channel is one of the most rewarding perks of being a decent and well-mannered Twitch streamer. Most streamers realize that a favour taken is a favour given. A few rotten apples may come by though, but as a whole, you will be treated kindly and with respect if you do the same to others.

Now, how do you actually network? There's no simple and correct answer to this. If you can manage (time-wise, financially, logistically) attending big events like PAX and TwitchCon remains one of the easiest ways to meet new people and establish strong, long-lasting relations with the members of the community. Again, don't just blatantly advertise your stream. That's even more repulsive in person, even if you have amazing facial features and a set of diamond white teeth. Treat these conventions as opportunities to meet the people you interact with and engage online in person. A smile and a firm, genuine handshake will often leave a much better impression than forcing your way into other streamers' Twitch chats and Twitter conversations.

Here's something else to keep in mind. Don't be stingy with your social currency. Follow other streamers, not just on Twitch, but on Twitter and other social media. Engage and interact with them and their audience. Drop them a shout-out on your own channel. All this and more will make it a tad bit easier to get a response once you send a PM and ask for help or collaboration.

Giveaways

Depending on your budget and overall financial situation, you may consider boosting your raw stats by doing giveaways. Before anything else, you have to understand that this can and probably will result in a lot of new viewers for the time being, or followers on Twitch, Twitter, Instagram and other social media channels if you organized an off-stream giveaway. However, only a small portion of these will stick around and actually watch your stream in the future. Most of these people will drop a follow only for a chance to win that shiny new Razer mouse you put up as a reward.

In terms of the type of giveaways, anything goes really. Offline giveaways hosted through Gleam.io are a standard more or less. They are certainly much better for pumping your follower stats across all social channels, but may result in little to no new viewers. Regardless, a portion of your new Twitter followers and YouTube subscribers will have your Tweets and uploads pop up on their feeds and notifications. A few may decide to genuinely check your stream out.

If you want a more direct approach, live giveaways that require people to watch your stream are a much better option for new streamers. Your 5-10 concurrent viewers may suddenly blow to 50, even 100. As these people will need to keep an eye on your stream to get info on the giveaway entries and winner announcements, seize this opportunity to try and engage with them. Play a chat mini-game – "continue the sentence" is always a good one. Some of them are surely going to interact because they're already watching you, so they may do it just out of boredom. Good. It means you can make your way into their mind-space. If you can win just 1 new viewer over, it's worth it.

Whatever you choose, don't rely on giveaways to be your source of new viewers. You don't want to become a "giveaway streamer" really, buying your viewers into coming by your stream just for a chance to win some rewards.

The art of the title

Coming up with a title that will capture attention and draw in new viewers is a valuable toolbox in every streamer's toolbox, no matter how big or small the channel is. Marketing gurus and agencies have spent decades meticulously studying and analyzing the titles that work best in any given circumstance. There are hundreds of books about marketing and advertising out there that can help you out come up with amazing titles.

CA$HVERTISING is probably the best choice if you are not familiar with the matter. It's written in an appealing, easy to digest way that demystifies and breaks down the power of advertising to even the most gullible people out there. As a matter of fact, it's probably the only book you will ever need to write eyeball-poking titles for the rest of your life.

That said, here are a few quick and easy ways to fix your bland and boring stream titles:

1) Funny and witty titles will always win over generic ones, no question about it. It shows you have a sense of humour and are probably more than willing to make an effort to entertain your viewers. "Smacking grannies in GTA V" is much more appealing and provocative than "GTA V stream until 11PM", right? It can also be a simple wordplay, like "Mindcraft Warcraft" or "Dark Souls bowls". You can always make fun of your own self "Come check me out suck

hard in Mario Kart!" And if you are skilled at the game, "Top 3 in the world, yeah baby! Let's go for No. 1!" will always work

2) Emotional appeal and pushing the "hot buttons" works wonders in some situations. For example, a new game was just launched in your genre of choice. You grab it immediately and title your stream "Here's how to kill it in GAME_NAME". What this does is creates a strong emotional pull towards finding out how to get better in a brand new game. Be careful about making false promises though – this is merely an idea. And if there's any particular game experiencing a rough patch, slam it down with it "GAME_NAME is driving me nuts. Care to join?!"

3) Numbers. Us humans have a strange propensity to quantify everything. Our brains are constantly searching for ways to distribute everything into proper sections and categories. Numbers represent a structured and precise hierarchy. Including numbers in your headlines works like a charm. "12+ winstreak in Fortnite tonite! Can we get to 15?!" is much more specific than "Winning every Fortnite match today!" Don't overdo it though. Ones, tens, hundreds and maybe thousands are good to go, so your 9, 35, 463 and 1087 will work, but anything above that requires additional processing on the part of your potential viewers. Don't drive her/him away by dropping millions in titles.

4) Powerful title starters. Without any particular order, you are almost guaranteed to capture more attention if your title starts with some of these:

- FREE
- NEW
- AT LAST
- THIS
- ANNOUNCING
- WARNING!
- JUST RELEASED
- NOW
- HERE'S
- THESE
- WHICH OF
- FINALLY
- LOOK
- PRESENTING
- INTRODUCING
- HOW
- AMAZING
- DO YOU
- WOULD YOU
- CAN YOU
- IF YOU
- STARTING TODAY

Variations can work as well. The point is to get the potential viewers to stop and read the rest of the title. If you have a strong message that follows after one of the starters above, your titles will generate more interested and draw in more viewers.

5) The question words, Why, Where, When, How, What... They imply a need for response and spark curiosity in our inquisitive minds. They trigger a response in our psyche. Don't shy away from controversy either. "Why are Hearthstone streamers drunkards?" is risky, but valid choice. Much better than "Playing Hearthstone, join me" anyway. "How can Blizzard still charge for this nonsense!" will send more than a few heads spinning your direction. "WOW Twitch raid party! Join us" provides no incentive for new viewers on the other hand. Why would they even want to join you when they don't even know you?

To "DRAMA", OR NOT?

There's no shortage of polarizing personalities and drama-queens on Twitch. Some go as far as instigating controversies and scandals around them to garner more attention to themselves. Without questioning the ethics and morality of adopting negative behavioural patterns, drama is as much a part of Twitch as webcams are.

Streamers and viewers alike constantly engage in proverbial *d**k* measuring contests with each other. "Oh I have more viewers", "Well, I have more followers, deal with it" Some of it is scripted and pre-planned. Some beefs are real though. Regardless of your own intention, you might catch yourself in the whirlwind of Twitch drama.

It can start off from something as stupid as someone asking you: "Do you think STREAMER_NAME is pretty?" If you say no, trolls will blow it out of water claiming you said the streamer in question is ugly. If you say yes, the same trolls will say that you have romantic feelings for the said person. In either case, you won't come out unscathed.

It boils down to one question – can you handle the notoriety and negative publicity? Some people can. However, it takes a person with a few extra layers of thick skin to handle the constant heat.

SOCIAL MEDIA AND EXPANDING YOUR REACH

In this day and age, if you are not active on Twitter, Instagram, Facebook and Snapchat, you are unnecessarily lowering your reach potential. Just as much as you want to engage and interact with people on Twitch, you will want to establish connections and relations on these social media platforms. You have to have presence on every major social media platform out there.

Twitter is great to send out short announcements and news about you and your channel and your brand. Instagram is the king of personal brand building. Let your followers gain a bit more insight into your life and they will be hooked even more.
Facebook doesn't work for everyone, but if you can establish a partnership relation with one of the popular Facebook brands that post regular viral content, you can get a lot of exposure for very little investment.
If you attract a bit younger demographic, you don't want to ignore Snapchat either. Silly is the new norm for the young generation of today, so lay out all of your wonderful weirdness for the world to see.

Then there is YouTube of course. The video giant still has a firm grip over online video format. However, it's a tough place to be and compete in. Even if you are just uploading your past streams in raw format, it is still a considerable effort to build and maintain the channel. Competition is massive and fierce. It's really hard to stand out, probably even harder than on Twitch. However, once the videos are up there, they are almost guaranteed to remain available virtually forever. If you are consistent with your uploads, the YouTube algorithm will invariably favour your videos over time, so they will pop up in recommended videos on the side more often and will start generating views.

YouTube has also made efforts to expand their brand into live-streaming akin to Twitch. If you want to absolutely maximize your stream reach and get exposed to dozens of different platforms, check out Restream.io. Among others, it allows you to stream to both Twitch and YouTube Gaming simultaneously, without putting any extra strain on your hardware and Internet connection. It's worth checking out at least.

CAN I ASK A FAVOR?

If you enjoyed this book, found it useful or otherwise then I would really appreciate it if you would post a short review on Amazon. I do read all the reviews personally so that I can continually write what people are wanting.

If you would like to leave a review then please visit the link below:

Thanks for your support!

39311928R00039

Made in the USA
San Bernardino, CA
19 June 2019